For Those Who Crave
Deeper Intimacy with God

25 DATES WITH GOD:
Volume Two
Courting Spiritual Intimacy

Cover Photo: © ibush - Fotolia.com
Interior Chapter Graphics: © Pavel Sevcov- Fotolia.com
Cover Design by: Hope River Arts

Please exercise safety and caution when following any of the date
plans in this book. Author and Publisher assume no liability for
activities engaged in by readers of this book.

Published in the United States of America

ISBN-13: 978-1-946344-03-8

ISBN-10: 1-946344-03-6

First Edition 2018

TABLE OF CONTENTS

1 Peter 1:8-9
"Though you have not seen Him,
you love Him;
and even though you do not see Him now,
you believe in Him and are
filled with an inexpressible and glorious joy,
for you are receiving the end result
of your faith,
the salvation of your souls."

Welcome Back to Dates With God

𝒥 am so glad you're back for more. More dates, more romance, more time with the One who wants to continue that head-over-heels love relationship with you: our One and Only, Divine God.

I hope by now you've completed the first volume's dates. It's time to go out again. This installment is called *Courting Spiritual Intimacy*.

Just like last time, I invite you to make "dating" part of your love story with God. Go on a journey through the pages to come. Enjoy more dates that create and foster intimacy between you and your Creator. He loves us so much. He wants to spend time with us. He is not distant.

I hope by the end of this book you will continue to know this is true at the deepest parts of your heart and soul. I hope you will also grow in faith, in intimacy, and in the ability to sense His voice and companionship.

Let's review how this works before you get started. (If you don't need a review, move straight to Date 1 and get this date party started.)

At the beginning of each date, I will give you a short guideline:

Location:
Supplies:
Reading:

Up front I will let you know what location to choose. Sometimes that may be as simple as "a quiet place." Other times, I'll get specific.

I'll also let you know what supplies to bring, like a journal, a Bible, art supplies, a camera. (Always assume you should bring this book with you, even if you leave it in the car sometimes. I won't include that on the list.)

Some dates require you to read the chapter in advance. The others you will read the chapter during the date. You just need to get to the place with the supplies outlined, then start the chapter once you're settled in.

Here are just a few additional guidelines. When experiencing these dates with God, I encourage you to set aside electronics that are not specifically needed for the date. For safety, when away from home, bring your phone. But consider airplane mode or, at the very least, use silent and keep it out of sight.

Spend time with the One you're with, without letting the outside world distract you. Treat God as you *should* treat a human date. For example, not letting your phone pull your attention at the dinner table.

You will need a camera, which is often our phone. Try to make sure you're not checking email or social networking sites, or texting and taking calls during your set-apart time with God.

I'd love for you to take selfies or photos of sites God shows you while out on dates. These photos will tie into a future date. Plus, I want you to have something to share with the rest of us if you choose to participate through the hashtag:

#dateswithGod

If you use Twitter, also tag our handle: @purplepenworks.

To join the fun, share pictures, insights, or anything you want about God encountering you on these dates.

Try to use just one journal for your dates so the notes you write during past dates will be with you. (If you already filled up that journal with Volume 1, start a fresh one.)

I want you recording memories, moments, words said between yourself and God. Yes, I do mean that. Expect two-way communication. If you feel like the Holy Spirit speaks something to your heart, write it down. Capture your memories together.

Ready to venture into your heavenly courtship? Let's move on to Volume 2, Date 1.

Date 1
Divinely Courting

Location: A quiet place at home
Supplies: A journal
Reading: Read chapter during your date

I hope you are as excited as I am to start the second round of this intimate courtship with God.

Start this date at home. If you get a chance to be alone, maybe share a quiet dinner—just you and God—with this book and your journal at your side. Maybe even light a candle. Turn on some soft praise music in the background. (I like some of those instrumental worship CDs too.)

If your only time to get alone at home with a meal is an early breakfast, go for it.

Whether you are married or single, I'm sure you have heard of the old school dating term "courting." A young man would be intentional about his pursuit of a young lady. Sometimes, he'd ask for permission to pursue her from her family. He certainly wasn't off courting many young ladies; he was focused on just one. It was a much different way to approach dating than how things are today with many young people.

My beloved husband, Chris, handled our courtship in a respectful, old-fashioned way. He made his intentions clear: he wanted to date me for the purpose of deciding if we should get married. He wouldn't be dating anyone else. He would be in communication with my parents as our relationship progressed. (He asked my dad for permission to propose. My sister and mother took the opportunity that day to help him plot the proposal.) He kept our relationship respectful and within God's intimacy boundaries for a couple before marriage. It was a romantic and delightful time in our history.

For you, in this journey, you are also focusing on the one and only God. You are not dating other gods. Your intimate affections are focused solely on *the one true God*. To make this clear, this is the God of the Holy Bible, the One who sent His only Son Jesus to die for us and for our sins.

God is the pursuer of our hearts. He craves intimacy with us. But He doesn't encroach on our free will. He wants an invitation to intimacy. He wants to know He's about to go on a date with someone who actually *wants* to go on a date with Him. (Don't we all get that? There's nothing like being on a date with someone who is clearly not into you.) Thankfully, just the fact that you have picked up this book is a signal to God that you want this type of relationship with Him.

We can court deeper spiritual intimacy with Him by invitation. An open and willing heart. By making Him a priority and setting apart this time.

Hopefully, you enjoyed the first 25 dates and you are ready for the next 25. I know I am.

Just like in the first volume, this date is for a check-in. You will write a journal entry that you will look back on during Date 25 to see how far you've grown since this moment in time.

Hopefully, your relationship has grown deeper since the first entry of Volume 1. Answer the following types of questions in that journal you've set apart for your *Dates With God* adventure:

- How do I feel about my relationship with God today? Do I feel close to Him or distant? Where is it strong and where can it improve?
- Are there any sin issues standing between us getting closer? Anything I need to confess to get the slate wiped clean so I can

be back in right fellowship with Him?
- Where do I hope to be by the end of this book, after going on 25 new dates with God?

Take your time with this entry. Be honest. God knows your heart anyway. It'll provide a good launching pad. Good relationships thrive in honesty.

I'm excited you are here. Let's continue on this path to court greater spiritual intimacy.

Date 2
Be Still

Location: A comfortable, quiet place to sit, preferably in nature by water. Ex. a waterfall, a beach, a lake.
Supplies: A blanket or beach towel, a journal
Reading: Read chapter during your date

If you are anything like me, "being still" doesn't come easily to you. I'm probably the most fidgety person I know.

As a kid, I was such a chatterbox that my mom played a game every parent would understand. She called it "The Silent Game." Here are the rules: Everyone immediately shuts their mouths and the first person to talk or make a sound loses. Of course, I lost. I lost *a lot*. Those stifled giggles eventually broke through.

When my nephews are being loud during dice games or cards or dominoes, my sister and I occasionally play the same game with them. They enjoy the competition until one of us cracks up. They make faces at us, trying to get us to laugh. Those few moments of peace and quiet are nice on the ears. (Not that my sister and I don't occasionally add our own loud game playing to the equation. Just ask Dad!)

How often do we come before God and talk the whole time without sitting to just be still?

Or, how often do we drown ourselves in busyness, unable to just quiet our minds and be silent before Him?

I'm sure you've heard the often-quoted verse, Psalm 46:10a: "Be still and know that I am God."

- Being still before God is a way to know Him.
- Being still before Him allows us to get out of the driver's seat and let Him take control.
- Being still takes our surrender.

Remember the story of Mary and Martha on the day Jesus visited their home?

Luke 10:38-42

"As Jesus and His disciples were on their way, He came to a village where a woman named Martha opened her home to Him.

39 She had a sister called Mary, who sat at the Lord's feet listening to what He said. 40 But Martha was distracted by all the preparations that had to be made. She came to Him and asked, 'Lord, don't you care that my sister has left me to do the work by myself? Tell her to help me!' 41 'Martha, Martha,' the Lord answered, 'you are worried and upset about many things, 42 but few things are needed — or indeed only one. Mary has chosen what is better, and it will not be taken away from her.'"

Wow. Mary has chosen what is better.

To sit. To be still.

To rest at the feet of Jesus.

Martha thought she was making the more righteous choice. But Jesus highlighted Mary's choice as better.

For this date, settle on your blanket or beach chair or on a rock by the water. I don't want you to be concerned if Jesus speaks today.

I want you to enjoy the peace and quiet. To listen to the sounds of nature around you. The waterfall, the lapping waves. Whatever is near you.

Sit. Listen. Breathe.

That's all you have to do.

We take so little time these days to just sit, be still, and listen to the sounds around us. Those sounds are usually drowned out by traffic, televisions, radios, barking dogs, and other people. Rarely do we get to just listen to the silence.

It may feel strange at first, but I have a feeling you'll be refreshed when your time is up.

If you sense the Lord wants to whisper something to you, take out that journal and write it down. However, don't ask Him to speak. Don't try to pray. We have plenty of other dates for that. Don't feel like either of you has to speak. Like a spouse or a close friend who you can drive amicably down the road with in silence, sit in silence with Jesus today.

My prayer is you will leave this date feeling refreshed, knowing you just enjoyed a quiet and peaceful time with the Lord.

Date 3
A Date with the Word

Location: A quiet place, preferably outside, like a park
bench or picnic table
Supplies: A journal, a Bible, Internet connection (ex.
through a phone or tablet)
Reading: Read chapter during your date

*I*f you wrote an autobiography, wouldn't you want
someone to get to know you by reading it? How
would you feel if the person you loved never picked
it up, never read a word?

Intimacy comes through *knowing*. And while it
may not seem like the most "romantic" activity, we
get to know the Lord by reading His Word. This is a
continuation of the Bible Roulette Date in Volume 1
with one main difference. Those were isolated verses

you felt led to read at random. This is looking at what God wants to share in a larger piece.

Today, when people quote Scripture, it's often out of context. They quote a verse that means something to them, but they haven't read the entire passage to understand its full meaning.

Let's admit it. Some stand-alone Scriptures sound better when they're not in context. They sound better quoted by themselves.

One example is Jeremiah 29:11. People love to quote this verse. I've done it myself. You know the one:

Jeremiah 29:11
"'For I know the plans I have for you,' declares the Lord, 'plans to prosper you and not to harm you, plans to give you hope and a future.'"

I've seen that verse on coffee cups, bookmarks, decorative signs, portions inscribed on pens. Why not? It's a completely lovely promise.

What some people don't realize is that this verse is only part of a speech Jeremiah gave to the Jewish people exiled in Babylon. It's a mix of comfort *and a reprimand*. It's not *only* a "comfort" verse of happy thoughts about future plans coming to pass. Not even close.

It doesn't bother me that people read it today as

if it still applies to us. What bothers me is they quote it by itself without verse 13. The one that contains a key piece of instruction. To get to this great plan of God, we must seek Him with all of our hearts.

There's even an isolated verse in Job that I like for this book's intimacy theme:

Job 29:4
"Oh, for the days when I was in my prime, when God's intimate friendship blessed my house."

I love that verse. I would welcome God's intimate friendship into my house any day. But I have to admit the rest of the chapter is rather sad, as Job reflects on happier times in his life.

For today's date, I'd like you to choose a longer section of scripture. Some potential choices include:

- Matthew 5-7 (The Sermon on the Mount)
- Galatians 5-6
- 1 John 3-4

I also suggest the option of reading 2 Samuel 22. Even though it's just one chapter, it's a little longer than most. I love this one as a demonstration of God's fierce love and protection.

If you really have a lot of time you could consider one of the smaller books that has four to six chapters each, like Philippians or Colossians.

See what you can learn about God and His love through this date. Let Him lead you to which section you should choose.

If you arrive at a common verse, see if you get further insights into what those verses mean that you may not have realized before when reading them or quoting them out of context.

Take your time. It won't hurt to read a different translation after the first run through, just to see if another translation offers you additional insights.

During your reading of the chapters of the Bible, ask the Holy Spirit for insights into what His heart is for you to understand from this. If your Bible cross-references a section to help you understand the meaning of something, look up those verses as well.

This may take some time. But reading it during one date will help you fully remember the chapters as a whole. I'm not very good at remembering what I read. So doing this exercise in one sitting is helpful to get the most out of it.

If you enjoy this date, feel free to repeat it in the future with other sections of the Bible. What better way to get to know your date than diving head first into the Book He inspired to be written about Himself?

Date 4
The Pampering Date

Location: A bathroom and tub at home
Supplies: Bubble bath, candles, music device
Reading: Read chapter before your date

$\mathcal{D}$o you ever feel guilty for taking a break? For indulging in a few moments of pampering? Does it make you feel bad that you're not cooking, cleaning, working, spending time with others, spending time with God, or any of the other thousands of tasks on your to-do list?

Productivity drives us so much today. With my personality, I often feel bad about myself if I am not accomplishing something.

Marrying Chris changed some of that for me. One personality trait that is completely different is that Chris is far more laid back and enjoys a slower pace in life. I am a bit higher strung and driven and always in a hurry. I even wondered if this big difference between us would be a cause for conflict once we got married.

Thankfully, instead, we've seen a great effect:

I speed him up; he slows me down. It's a wonderful balance.

Sometimes, it's still hard for me to take time to enjoy the peace and quiet, that little bit of indulgence.

One important priority that should be on your to-do list is to spend time with God. What if you could do that *and* take a restful break for one of your dates? That sounds good to me. Spend time with God and pamper myself. Productive rest, right?

God loves rest; He created it. He even thought it was important enough to record as a full-on commandment in His Word. Rest on the Sabbath. I'm sure He knew we wouldn't take enough time for rest if we weren't instructed to. Even God rested!

Genesis 2:2-3
"By the seventh day God had finished the work He had been doing; so on the seventh day He rested from all His work. Then God blessed the seventh day and made it holy, because on it He rested from all the work of creating that He had done."

If God chose rest after hard work, what makes us think we don't need it?

When we moved into our new home in the Atlanta area, I was jazzed our master bathroom had a garden tub. I've never lived in a place with one of those. A large round tub, complete with armrests. I wondered if it would entice me to slow down enough at times to enjoy it.

Thankfully, it has. For Christmas our first year living there, I asked for bath bombs with a variety of essential oils, a cushy tub pillow for my back and head. Scented candles to use instead of harsh lighting, a Scentsy and an essential oils diffuser. And of course, I couldn't forget the bubble bath.

To help with pain I sometimes have in my legs, I wanted various types of Epsom salts. Having leg pain has slowed me down and even encouraged me to spend more time in this haven. It's not only physically renewing, it can be spiritually as well.

But what if time is short and it's hard to feel like you're indulging when so much needs to be done? Well, one item that should be on your list is spending time with God. So this is a great solution. Use this time as a date.

If you don't already have the supplies, try to buy a few items to help you feel pampered before you take this date. You don't need a garden tub. Any tub will do. At least get a candle or two, and bubble bath.

Then while filling in that tub, I'd like you to read over the following scriptures where God encourages peace, rest, taking a break, so you can go into this sweet and quiet time without guilt. I love how in these Scriptures, God encourages rest.

Matthew 11:28
"Come to Me, all you who are weary and burdened, and I will give you rest."

Psalm 55:6
"I said, 'Oh, that I had the wings of a dove! I would fly away and be at rest.'"

Isaiah 26:3
"You will keep in perfect peace those whose minds are steadfast, because they trust in You."

Psalm 23:2b-3a
"...He leads me beside quiet waters, He refreshes my soul."

Let the Lord refresh your soul now.

A last tip: You can listen to praise music during this bath. I like to do this because it makes me feel like I am hanging out with God without having to *do* anything. I can enjoy listening to encouraging or uplifting lyrics.

But if you prefer quiet, go right ahead. This is your time. Like on the "Be Still" date, being quiet is God's idea. It can be renewing as well.

You can take time during your bath to chat with God if you would like, while you have this set apart private time. But don't make it feel like work if you just need quiet. Plus, you don't have to pray the whole time. Just soak in His presence.

I'm sure it goes without saying...this is not the date for selfies. This one is just between you and God. Have fun and relax.

Date 5
Artistic Wonder

Location: A café, private table in or outside

Supplies: A sketch notebook, pad, or plain paper, colored pencils (or your preferred drawing and coloring supplies)

Reading: Read whole chapter before your date

As a writing professor, I often tell my students, "God is the greatest creative mind in the universe." It's a slogan I've put on screen savers. I love that we have access to the One who created creativity, who has more artistic talent than any of us. It's what makes writing fun. I can get into a groove where I feel like God is sitting right beside me, helping me write the right words. Or to bring form out of nothing (a.k.a. the blank page).

Many years ago, a 24-7 prayer room opened at a local church. It had so many fun, artistic stations to enjoy during prayer time.

One of those stations included sketchpads, crayons, colored pencils, paints, small canvases, and easels. Even I took out a pad and drew something cool. I didn't know what I would draw when I chose my sketchpad. I just sat prayerfully and waited until God's inspiration hit me for what to draw. I didn't need any real talent to participate.

Some people left their drawings behind for others to enjoy. So the prayer room became decorated with spiritual images.

I've attended many churches that engage in what they call "prophetic art." They have artists (who can actually paint or draw well) at the front on stage, often to the side of where the praise band or preacher is. They paint or draw throughout praise and worship or even during the whole sermon. You get to watch these drawings morph from nothingness into beautiful images. Some of those artists know in advance what they'll create. Some wait until the sermon or music begins to pray and ask God what He'd like to inspire them to paint.

A local church has a once-a-month night for healing prayer. You go to a praise and worship room while you wait for your turn to join prayer counselors for healing prayer. Once you go in that room, they have children and young adults at tables off to the side drawing or painting. The kids are not close enough to hear what you ask for during prayer. They paint small, 4-by-6 images. They ask God what to paint. Then they walk around the room and ask God, "Who is this for?" The child then hands that drawing to whomever the child feels should get it. Sometimes they offer a little word of encouragement or they tell you what they think it means. Other times they just say something like, "I feel like this is for you."

The first time we went, my husband and I were there to receive prayer about specific healing needs. When we were about to leave, a 12-year old child walked up to me and said, "God wants you to have this." The painting she made matched the request we'd prayed about. The picture showed the healed version of our answer to prayer. I was so blessed by this. Especially since the child didn't hear what we were praying for. It's like this 12-year old received a vision from God, drew it, then delivered it. Amazing, isn't it? I loved the look of faith on her face as she gave it to me. It felt like confirmation that those who'd prayed over me that night for healing and declared it would come were hearing God correctly. This drawing was further confirmation.

I love that God can use art to speak to us. And now I'd like you to use art to enjoy our time with God.

The Bible shares about various artistic people. One example is in Exodus 35:31-33:

> "And He has filled him with the Spirit of God, with wisdom, with understanding, with knowledge and with all kinds of skills—to make artistic designs for work in gold, silver and bronze, to cut and set stones, to work in wood and to engage in all kinds of artistic crafts."

In Volume 1 of *Dates With God*, I had you head to a café to use one of those adult coloring books. The lines were already there for you. For this date, I'd love for you to let your inner artist out in a more original way. One that allows God to inspire your art.

Draw something on a blank page. Don't feel like you have the talent to do so? Well, you get to join my club because I don't either.

This is not about drawing something you can frame for your wall or laminate as a bookmark. (Unless, of course, you want to.) This is more about praying, asking God what *He* would like you to draw, then putting it on the page. He doesn't care if you draw that perfectly crafted, chubby face of a cherub or trees that look like they belong in the forest, or a stunning sunset with all the right hues. He's not judging or grading. (Thankfully!)

The idea is to ask prayerfully what God would like you to draw today.

Wait on Him. He may lead you to a Bible verse first, then inspire a drawing to go with it. Or He may give you an idea for a picture first.

Either way, start drawing.

Once your picture is complete—if it wasn't first inspired by a verse—ask what verse goes with this image. Then write the caption. Keep it as a keepsake. Or if God so leads, give it away to someone He highlights. The choice is up to you.

I like the idea of doing this at a café, off at a private table, where it feels like a real date. I hope you also find it peaceful and relaxing.

Let that inner artist out, under the divine inspiration of the most Creative Being on the planet.

Date 6
Our Trustworthy One

Location: A quiet place
Supplies: Journal and pen
Reading: Read chapter during your date

$\mathcal{W}$hen I first thought about writing this devotional, I pondered how many dates to include in each installment. I'd thought of 30 or 31, but I didn't want to imply that we could do this every day in one month. The last thing women need is another reason to feel guilty, as if they're falling short.

I want these dates to be special, set aside moments with God that will take effort to carve out. A highlight (or two) of your week. A special date every day isn't practical.

So, then I got the idea of creating 25 dates. Right

after that, I felt led to read Psalm 25. Naturally, I've read it before but didn't know the reference. I'm going to quote it here in full. I want you to read it one time all the way through and then I'll give you an assignment to go back through and read it again.

Psalm 25
"In You, LORD my God,
I put my trust.
2 I trust in You;
do not let me be put to shame,
nor let my enemies triumph over me.
3 No one who hopes in You
will ever be put to shame,
but shame will come on those
who are treacherous without cause.
4 Show me Your ways, LORD,
teach me Your paths.
5 Guide me in Your truth and teach me,
for You are God my Savior,
and my hope is in You all day long.
6 Remember, LORD, Your great mercy
and love, for they are from of old.
7 Do not remember the sins of my youth
and my rebellious ways;
according to Your love remember me,
for You, LORD, are good.
8 Good and upright is the LORD;

therefore He instructs sinners in His ways.
9 He guides the humble in what is right
and teaches them His way.
10 All the ways of the LORD are loving
and faithful toward those who keep the
demands of His covenant.
11 For the sake of Your name, LORD,
forgive my iniquity, though it is great.
12 Who, then, are those who fear the
LORD? He will instruct them in the ways
they should choose.
13 They will spend their days in
prosperity, and their descendants will
inherit the land.
14 The LORD confides in those who fear
Him; He makes His covenant known to
them.
15 My eyes are ever on the LORD, for only
He will release my feet from the snare.
16 Turn to me and be gracious to me,
for I am lonely and afflicted.
17 Relieve the troubles of my heart
and free me from my anguish.
18 Look on my affliction and my distress
and take away all my sins.
19 See how numerous are my enemies
and how fiercely they hate me!

20 Guard my life and rescue me;

do not let me be put to shame,

for I take refuge in You.

21 May integrity and uprightness protect

me, because my hope, LORD, is in You.

22 Deliver Israel, O God,

from all their troubles!"

There is much to unpack in this Scripture. Looking at this Psalm shows how God can be everything we'd ever need. But it also highlights ways in which we may miss a portion of His personality that could be helpful to us.

So many things this prayer warrior asks for! He does so, based on who God is. What do you see in this passage? This Psalm covers many ways in which God can interact with us and why.

Next I'd like you to reread this Psalm, meditate on it, and ask God to show you insights about it and who He is, exploring questions like the following:

- Which traits of God highlighted in this chapter do I see at work in my life?
- Which ones feel dormant?
- Which ones would I like to experience?
- Is there anything that I feel inhibits me?
- How does this Psalm invite me to a place of deeper intimacy and romance with God?

Some parts of this chapter have an If-Then feeling to it, as if we have a responsibility on our end before God does His part. It could mean a need for obedience. It could mean trusting in His love for you more fully. Take a look at that on a deeper level as you journal about your second read of this passage. Record all insights He speaks to you about it.

Finally, ask God these last couple of questions and see if you sense an answer in your Spirit from Him:

- God, who do You want to be for me?
- Which parts of You am I not acquainted with yet that You'd like me to get to know?

God is worth getting to know deeper every day of our lives. One of His most admirable traits is trustworthiness. I'm thankful God proves Himself an expert in this area. I dare say He's the author of trust.

May we also strive to be trustworthy in our relationship with the Lover of Our Souls.

Date 7
The Serenade

Location: A private place at home

Supplies: A computer with an Internet connection, YouTube

Reading: Read whole chapter before your date

*Y*ou've seen the movies. The ones where the guy stands under the girl's window and serenades her. Sings a song, recites an original poem, quotes a sonnet, or plays a boom box over his head and sings along. Whatever the case may be, it always felt romantic. The idea is that someone would either learn a song or write their own lyrics to sing to the one whose heart they wanted to capture.

In this case, you've already captured God's

heart. You're not trying to win Him over for the first time. But you can romance Him, share your heart, and sing a song that delights Him. Once you get married, you don't stop romancing your husband, correct? (Or vice versa. My husband has written me at least seven love songs so far. His first debuted at our wedding reception.)

We can invite God's romantic presence with a song too. (Only we don't have to write that song unless we so desire.)

Psalm 30:4
"Sing the praises of the LORD, you His faithful people; praise His holy name."

Psalm 96:1
"Sing to the LORD a new song, sing to the LORD all the earth."

Psalm 100:1-2
"Shout for joy to the LORD, all the earth. Worship the LORD with gladness; come before Him with joyful songs."

God loves to be praised. He loves a joyful noise. And guess what? He doesn't even care if I can carry a tune and stay on key. Nope! This is not about our talent as singers. This date is about serenading Him with one love song. Which song that will be is up to you. I encourage you to pick a song you love, preferably a slow ballad. Get to know it before your grand serenade.

A great way to do this is get into that private place. Try to be where no one can hear you so you are uninhibited. Hop on YouTube and find the song, listen to it a few times so you can get to know it well, if you don't already.

Then stand up, get ready to hit the replay button, and serenade your God with a ballad. (We'll save the fast and fun songs for a future book installment, where a karaoke date will be. But this date is for that sweet serenade.) I want you to pick one song. Sing it more than once if you'd like.

For many years, one of my favorite songs to use during a serenade to God was *Inside Out* by Hillsong. More recently, after attending a Bethel Music concert where they were recording a new album, my favorite serenade song became *Starlight* by Amanda Cook. I had never heard it before the concert, but it caught my attention. It starts off quiet and slow then builds to such a beautiful place. Something in my heart stirred during that song. I wrote down a few lyrics so I could try to find it later, in case she'd sung it before in a service (since I knew the album wouldn't be out for a while at that time. It is out now.)

I found a live version from Bethel Church. I played that song over and over, soaking in its worshipful tune. And now it's become my favorite serenade song.

For you, find the one that feels right that you can halfway sing (or even if you can't, doesn't matter to God). Use the video that has lyrics on it, if you don't already know the words. You can also search for lyrics on lyric sites, if there isn't a video so you can sing the words to God. I prefer to use songs that have lyric videos so I can just look at the screen when needed. Do whatever works best for you.

The point is to sing a love song to the One who loves you wider, deeper, and higher than anyone else ever could.

Now, sing on!

Date 8
Your Spiritual Gifts

Location: At home or a place you have an Internet
    connection
Supplies: A laptop or desktop, printer, paper, pen
Reading: Read chapter during your date

$\mathcal{W}$e all have things we are good at, right? Natural
gifts and talents.

God has given each of us spiritual gifts too. It's
not within the scope of this book to teach about all of
them. For a complete study, I recommend my friend
Susan Rohrer's book series:

The Holy Spirit: Spiritual Gifts: Book 1 and *Book 2.*

Rohrer divides the Bible's spiritual gifts into
two basic categories in her series:

Power Gifts and Service Gifts.

It's likely that each of us have some, and not likely that we have all. (In fact, it's biblical that we don't have all of them so we need other people to make the body work as a whole.)

Before I take you to today's activity for your date, I'd like to quote a few passages of Scripture that name some of the gifts of the Spirit, just to refresh your memory on what they are. These verses won't list every gift, but they include many of them.

The first passage mostly mentions those power gifts. The second one (other than prophecy) lists some of the service gifts. The third one mentions the five-fold ministry gifts. I encourage you, as you read through these, jot down the list of gifts you see named here.

1 Corinthians 12: 1-11

"Now about the gifts of the Spirit, brothers and sisters, I do not want you to be uninformed. 2 You know that when you were pagans, somehow or other you were influenced and led astray to mute idols. 3 Therefore I want you to know that no one who is speaking by the Spirit of God says, 'Jesus be cursed,' and no one can say, 'Jesus is Lord,' except by the Holy Spirit. 4 There are different kinds of gifts, but the same Spirit distributes them. 5 There are different kinds of service, but the same Lord. 6 There are different kinds of working, but in all of them and in everyone it is the same God at work. 7 Now to each one the manifestation of the Spirit is given for the common good. 8 To one there is given through the Spirit a message of wisdom, to another a message of knowledge by means of the same Spirit, 9 to another faith by the same Spirit, to another gifts of healing by that one Spirit, 10 to another miraculous powers, to another prophecy, to another distinguishing between spirits, to another speaking in different kinds of tongues, and to still another the interpretation of tongues. 11 All these are the work of one and the same Spirit, and He distributes them to each one, just as He determines."

Romans 12:3-8
"For by the grace given me I say to every one of you: Do not think of yourself more highly than you ought, but rather think of yourself with sober judgment, in accordance with the faith God has distributed to each of you. 4 For just as each of us has one body with many members, and these members do not all have the same function, 5 so in Christ we, though many, form one body, and each

member belongs to all the others. 6 We have different gifts, according to the grace given to each of us. If your gift is prophesying, then prophesy in accordance with your faith; 7 if it is serving, then serve; if it is teaching, then teach; 8 if it is to encourage, then give encouragement; if it is giving, then give generously; if it is to lead, do it diligently; if it is to show mercy, do it cheerfully."

Ephesians 4:11-13

"So Christ Himself gave the apostles, the prophets, the evangelists, the pastors and teachers, 12 to equip his people for works of service, so that the body of Christ may be built up 13 until we all reach unity in the faith and in the knowledge of the Son of God and become mature, attaining to the whole measure of the fullness of Christ."

So, now that you've read some Scriptures naming the gifts, do you know what yours are? If you jotted down that list, you can put a star by any you think God may have given to you.

The next step of today's date is to take a spiritual gifts test.

Even if you think you know what your gifts are, it's fun to take a test, just to see how your answers match up. You may come to realize you have a gift you didn't know about, or didn't realize it was a spiritual gift.

This is why you need the Internet. I am not the author of any such gift test. But I can point you in the right direction toward two that are free online.

Lifeway Christian Resources has a good one that covers the service gifts and power gifts. I found it searching for "Discover Your Spiritual Gifts" and Lifeway's name in a search engine.

I also like the C. Peter Wagner test. (The closest one I found online free was called "Wagner Modified HOUTS Questionnaire.")

Since website names change all the time, I don't want to supply direct links. Both tests offer a great explanation of spiritual gifts and definitions. They offer scripture references as well.

So, find your test. Don't read the test in advance or it could skew your results.

Print, take the test, and score.

The more you know about your spiritual gifts, the more intimate you can become with the One you're dating. After you get your results, ask God where you are already using those gifts. Then ask if there are ways He'd like you to use those gifts that you haven't already.

Then go out and serve with gladness, knowing the God of the universe is right beside you, holding your hand, equipping you with His precious gifts.

Date 9
Reach Out With Love

Location: To be determined by activity chosen
Supplies: None
Reading: Read whole chapter before your date

Can you say, "Out of Cheryl's Comfort Zone"? For the introverted girl who doesn't completely enjoy talking to strangers, any volunteer work — especially with people I don't know — is a stretch for me.

Don't be like me. Don't skip this date because it's not comfortable.

Seriously. Don't just move on to the next chapter. I know it's tempting. But you could miss a special time with God if you bypass it.

For this date, I'm encouraging us to look

beyond ourselves, reach out to someone else in need, and give of our time.

Not just our money. Our time.

There is no shortage of Scriptures that encourage us to help others.

James 1:27
"Religion that God our Father accepts as pure and faultless is this: to look after orphans and widows in their distress and to keep oneself from being polluted by the world."

Psalm 82:3
"Defend the weak and the fatherless; uphold the cause of the poor and the oppressed."

Isaiah 58:7
"Is it not to share your food with the hungry and to provide the poor wanderer with shelter—when you see the naked, to clothe them, and not to turn away from your own flesh and blood?"

Matthew 25:40
"...Truly I tell you, whatever you did for one of the least of these brothers and sisters of Mine, you did for Me."

There are plenty of worthy causes that we can give money to and let the monetary gift be the end of the story. But there's something about giving our time that makes it a completely different experience. I believe the Bible encourages both types of giving.

Can you imagine if someone asked you out on a date and instead of going with you just handed you money to pay for it? They didn't want to go on the date with you. Not an exciting night out, is it?

Let's not do that here. Let's participate in full and with our willing hearts.

For this date, I'd like you to find one thing you'd like to do as a volunteer. Jesus served His Father with a willing heart, always open to doing what He saw the Father doing. (John 5:19)

So, where do you start? First off, to prep for this date, you pray. Big surprise, right? Ask God to point out something special that He'd like you to get involved with. This can be something that uses a special talent you have or it can be something you've never done before. Let God help you choose. You never know what experience He may have in mind for you.

Personally, I like any volunteer work to be 100% away from writing or filmmaking. I spend more than full-time hours of my life working and writing. I don't want volunteer work to feel like an extension of my job. You may have a different preference there.

While volunteer work blesses those we help, it also blesses us even if that's not the motive when we go into it.

The sources I use to check for volunteer opportunities are my church or my community magazines and websites. Some of my business networking groups also have opportunities.

Where we live outside Atlanta, we have more than enough soup kitchens, opportunities to work with special needs kids or adults, tutoring, or helping with special events in our cute downtown area. (For example, churches band together and put on holiday-themed parties or carnivals for kids at various times of year.)

A nearby police department puts on a charity event for Christmas where we can take underprivileged kids shopping for gifts. (We walk them through the store, help them pick out a gift on budget, and make sure it's actually for them. Seriously, a lot of these kids ask for gifts that you find out are for their big sisters or little brothers. Or in a heartbreaking way, sometimes they just ask for toilet paper as their gift. Thankfully, the police department hands out those sorts of necessities so the kids can still get a toy.)

One recent ad that caught my attention in one of our local magazines was a battered women's shelter. I was in the middle of writing a screenplay, based on a book about one woman's journey through her abusive marriage. So this ad caught my heart. It also was a volunteer op that I have to admit was squarely in Cheryl's Comfort Zone.

It was for Thanksgiving. Some women had taken their children to this shelter and needed help putting together a special Thanksgiving meal. They gave us a list of items they wanted for that meal and treats their kids had asked for. I went shopping with the lists, carefully checking off many items. I made it a prayerful date as I asked God to help me pick out what these kids and mothers would like. I prayed for the ones who would receive these items.

I went by the shelter to bring all the food and treats. Due to the confidential nature of the shelter, I was only allowed to meet with staff and not residents to bring the food.

It would have been easier to donate money from afar. Instead, I made it a little date with God.

One of the coolest events that happens all over the country yearly is Tim Tebow's *Night to Shine*, where special needs children get to walk the red carpet into their own version of a prom. A friend of mine, who is a make-up artist for movies, volunteered her time to make up the ladies. What a way to help them feel special! I cite this example, even though it isn't mine, because it's a great way for one to integrate a talent or gift they already have in what they shared with others.

I have served in various soup kitchens. I like

that because you have a specific task to do. Something to do with your hands. It makes being friendly and talking to strangers less awkward.

Maybe you don't have that shyness, introvert problem like I do. If so, you'd be great as the one who mingles in the crowd, going table to table at the soup kitchen, sitting with families and talking to them. (My husband is much better at that than I am.)

Once you choose what your volunteer event will be, make a date of it. Before you go, ask God to show Himself to you during the event. Let Him know you are open to sharing a word of encouragement with someone, if He points someone out to you. Ask Him just to be present, to go with you, to protect you, to give you the boldness you need for the event. Then during the event, check in with God from time to time. Ask Him if there's anything He wants you to see or do.

I volunteered as a tutor at a group home, serving as a "special friend" to a boy who had emotional issues and struggled with reading. I asked God what I could do to share with him about Jesus, but without being too obvious. This wasn't a Christian group home; it was state run. That's when I felt like God inspired me to bring my children's book that I co-wrote with Frank Peretti and Sharon Lamson. It's called *The Wild and Wacky Totally True Bible Stories*. One of my tasks was to help this boy improve his reading. So we'd sit down during my visits, and I'd have him read through kids' Bible stories before we'd play basketball—the prize after cooperating with the tutoring portion of our meeting.

I'll admit. Sometimes he'd get rambunctious. One day he decided to yell the story of Noah at the top of his lungs across the courtyard. I was afraid I'd get caught for "smuggling" in my Bible stories. But thankfully, no one noticed.

Keep in mind this isn't a date you have to do alone. Feel free to enjoy with a friend, a spouse, or one of your kids or church groups.

My husband and I signed up to build turkey baskets with our Young Marrieds group at church and returned to serve food to their young people at a service. We also participated with our small group in an event to benefit single mothers. So these are just some of the types of ideas you could consider.

After you do your chosen event, complete the date by writing an entry in your *Dates With God* journal. Share about your experience, where you felt God in your presence during the event and what you liked about it. Maybe even reflect on any part of it that felt uncomfortable and ask God how to overcome that, so you are not shy about doing things like this in the future.

Maybe also write a list of other activities you'd like to do. Make this a regular date.

Date 10
Back to the Garden

Location: A quiet place in a botanical garden, or a local park with flowers and beauty. Set up a blanket or sit on a bench in the garden itself and take a break.

Supplies: A picnic lunch or money to buy lunch if they have a café, a journal, a Bible, a phone with an Internet connection to YouTube

Reading: Read chapter during your date

Sometimes, I wish we could go back.

Before sin.

Back to when communication with God was as simple as walking beside Him in a garden.

The truth is, we can have that simplicity. We

can walk with Him and hear His voice. We just need to take that time out in the garden to be alone with Him. To have a clean slate, nothing between us. And that's the heart of what this book series is about. Getting us alone with God.

Back in the garden.

The Garden of Eden, before the fall.

What a concept. Can you imagine what it was like back then when Adam and Eve just walked with God in harmony? They chatted like friends. There was no difficulty in sharing with one another, in carrying on an amicable conversation.

Things changed after sin entered their world in the Garden. It messed up that intimate "garden" experience.

Let's remember that we can be redeemed. Our sins are forgiven, if we have confessed our sinfulness and accepted Jesus Christ as our personal Savior, the only way to forgiveness and reconciliation with God.

When I was little, I would spend time with my grandfather at the organ. He'd play various hymns on that stand-up Magnus organ, the kind with the little buttons with letters above them to use for accompanying chords.

Dado, as we loved to call him, had a favorite song he often played:

In the Garden.

Allow me to share those lyrics as penned by C. Austin Miles in 1913. I'd love for you to read these lyrics slowly first. Then if you have your phone, pull up a video on YouTube, listen to the song. (You can choose a more classic version, like the one by George Beverly Shea, or other artists like the ones by Elvis Presley or Johnny Cash or Loretta Lynn, or more modern ones like Alan Jackson or Brad Paisley. There are many options to choose from.)

As you listen to the song, close your eyes and try to picture the scene, the imagery the author painted with words:

In the Garden

I come to the garden alone
While the dew is still on the roses
And the voice I hear falling on my ear
The Son of God discloses.

And He walks with me and He talks with me,
And He tells me I am His own;
And the joy we share as we tarry there,
None other has ever known.

He speaks and the sound of His voice,
Is so sweet the birds hush their singing,
And the melody that He gave to me
Within my heart is ringing.

And He walks with me and He talks with me,
And He tells me I am His own;
And the joy we share as we tarry there,
None other has ever known.

I'd stay in the garden with Him
Though the night around me be falling,
But He bids me go; through the voice of woe
His voice to me is calling.

And He walks with me and He talks with me,
And He tells me I am His own;
And the joy we share as we tarry there,
None other has ever known.

Now, write a journal entry, a love letter to God about the ways in which you'd like more intimate, closer communication with Him like it must have been in the Garden of Eden.

Ask Him if anything has been getting in the way of your direct line to Him and what you should do about it.

You may have come to the garden today without a specific agenda. But this is a date I encourage you to repeat as often as needed. And sometimes, you may have a prayer agenda. You may have specific needs to lift to God in prayer or even seek answers about. Sometimes, getting away in the quiet of the garden can be the best way to hear Him.

Years ago, when Chris and I were dating, I wasn't in that place where I knew with 100% certainty where our relationship was going. I wanted to pray about it and to seek God's heart.

So I went to a botanical garden in Arcadia, California, called the Arboretum. I took a journal and a Bible. I found a cute bench by the water, near one of the gardens. It was nicely secluded from most foot traffic.

I penned my prayers, my concerns, and even my hopes. I welcomed God to speak. I can honestly say, that day, I felt like God said Chris was a door He was opening for me. And that day, all He was asking was for me to be open to it. He wasn't giving me a definite yes or no just yet. (He knew I wasn't ready to hear it. That came later.) But God gently guided me forward. So a few days later, I knew I could get on a plane to visit my family and Chris and that this was a relationship worth exploring. God gave me a peace about it that day in the garden.

So my encouragement to you is, any time you crave intimate fellowship or even if you need to seek God for guidance, go back to the garden. Maybe you can't always escape to a literal botanical garden like you have on this date. Find a place you can be peaceful and quiet and have your heart inclined toward Him.

For today, after you have your quiet time (and

perhaps a picnic lunch), spend the rest of your date walking through the garden or park, enjoying the sites, the flowers and God's great artistry. Take time to appreciate His incredible creativity in crafting each type. Also take time to enjoy the birds. Talk to God about what you enjoy about His creation. Take pictures of beautiful flowers and yourself to save for your *Dates With God* scrapbook.

And remember to take that peaceful calm you feel now home with you. Any time it seems to evaporate, return to the garden in your spirit.

Date 11
On the Altar

Location: A chapel or mission, or your own church
sanctuary
Supplies: A pen, journal
Reading: Read whole chapter before your date

In my script and novel for *Never the Bride*, my lead
character Jessie has a control problem. (Any
similarity to my real life is purely coincidental,
right?) She likes to be in control of her love story and
the pen she uses to compose it. But after she accuses
God of being asleep on the job of writing her love
story for her, God shows up to face those charges. In
the flesh, looking her age and adorable.

God's challenge for her is to let Him write her
story. For her to surrender that pen. The pen she's

used her whole life to journal about all the ways she'd like her love life to go.

Can you imagine if God showed up to ask you to surrender the pen of your life? Well, in many ways, He already has. He asks us to trust Him. He asks us to believe that He knows best no matter what happens in our lives.

God wants our surrender; He wants us to trust Him with control of our lives.

Let's just admit it. Sometimes, it's hard. We like to control our lives. And no doubt, God welcomes us many times into the decision making process. He gave all of us unique personalities and none of us are acting as robots. He also gave us free will.

Yet, in spite of that free will, there is something beautiful about when a child of God voluntarily offers Him that pen. He loves it when we let Him take over an area of life where we want His divine intervention. Where we know we must give up the grip of control.

This is an action I took when I was single. I was copying Jessie from my script and novel.

In May 2010, I was in the middle of one of those heartbreaks. A hope in a relationship that I wanted wasn't materializing. I decided to go on a retreat with God alone.

In California, finding retreat centers is easy around missions. If you don't live on the west coast, it may be harder to find places like that.

While there, I felt inspired to take one of my beloved purple pens and leave it on the altar. I had a hard time not laughing through the process. I didn't want anyone around me to know what I was doing. This was a private moment between God and me.

I sat in the pew for a long time and wrote out a prayer with that purple pen about how I was tired of doing things my way. I wanted and welcomed God's intervention, no matter what. Then I walked down the middle aisle of the mission church. (No, that wasn't symbolic or anything.)

When I arrived at the altar, I sat on the little steps leading up to the platform. I prayed a bit more and then told God He could have the pen.

After leaving it there, I walked out, not intending to use it again myself. It was God's now.

Ironically, one year later—to the exact day—I was walking down the aisle toward my groom.

So, how about you? Is there an area you would like to voluntarily surrender to God?

This may be an area that is going completely wrong. It may be an area that hasn't begun yet and you want it to go right. So you preemptively give up control. Only you know what you're going through right now and what area of your life you'd like to surrender.

In this case, I'm not talking about the big surrender: salvation. I'm assuming if you are reading this book you've probably already surrendered your life to God. That you believe Jesus Christ is the one true way to heaven, that He died for your sins and you are redeemed by His grace if you ask, and surrender your heart to Him. If you haven't, then that is something that you may want to consider taking care of right away. (John 3:16 and the whole Gospel of John are good sections to read first.)

For this date, I want you to choose an area of your life that you haven't fully surrendered to God. One that you'd like to voluntarily give over to God, for Him to do with as He pleases.

Are you waiting on God to write your love story?

Are you struggling with infertility and hoping that God will help you and your spouse become parents?

Are you waiting on an emotional healing, a physical healing?

Are you praying for a job or career change? A move?

Maybe you're not even sure what you should surrender, but you'd like to take this date to ask God what He'd like you to surrender. That's okay too!

Choose something that you feel you either desire to turn over to Him or that you've tried to do on your own and so far it hasn't worked out. Or go into this fresh, ready for God to guide you and point something out.

Then take a pen. Not just any old pen, but a pen that you like. Maybe a pen you've used to journal with. Find a chapel, or a mission, or a church you can visit that is open to the public. (Catholic churches tend to be unlocked during the day. Just go during a time they're not having mass.) Have prayer time in their pews. And then, afterward, walk up to the altar and leave behind that pen. It will be a ceremonial and symbolic occasion between you and God. (Hopefully, no one will be around to see what you're doing.)

Leave it on the altar. (Sneak a picture of that pen for your scrapbook.) Then trust and wait on God to move in the area you've surrendered. It may be soon. It may take a long time. But whenever the urge comes to steal the pen back (because you feel like God is not at work or taking too long) remember this date you spent at the church or mission. Remember that pen on the altar. The one you can't return to retrieve anyway.

So, plan that time to go out and do this. Bring your journal and special pen. Then wait and see what God will write on your behalf. I have no doubt His story will be far and above any story you could write for yourself.

Let me leave you with lyrics from a portion of an inspirational song, *I Surrender All*, by Judson W. Van DeVenter (1896).

I Surrender All

All to Jesus I surrender,
All to Him I freely give;
I will ever love and trust Him,
In His presence daily live.

I surrender all,
I surrender all;
All to Thee, my blessed Savior,
I surrender all.

All to Jesus I surrender,
Humbly at His feet I bow;
Worldly pleasures all forsaken,
Take me, Jesus, take me now.

All to Jesus I surrender,
Make me, Savior, wholly Thine;
Let me feel the Holy Spirit,
Truly know that Thou art mine.

It was a privilege to spend this time with God. To walk away from that altar feeling like God could be trusted with this important area of my life. I felt like our relationship grew in intimacy from this act of surrender.

Date 12
Sing Over Me

Location: A quiet place, preferably at home in a private room or a place to go on a prayer walk

Supplies: A journal, phone with Internet connection to YouTube, or music player

Reading: Read opening paragraph before your date to determine timing, then read full chapter before the date

$\mathcal{T}$his date is to be shared with God during a time you are going through a rough patch. This could be a difficult day or a hard season. So if you are in a good season, set this date aside and hold it for a time when you need some encouragement from the Lord.

I've had rough seasons in my life. Sometimes,

getting away with God on prayer walks was the only thing that kept me going.

Music was often key to God ministering to my spirit, helping me return to wholeness and wellness. I'd load up a play list of encouraging songs that spoke to my situation on my MP3 player and listen to them out on a walk. Or I'd play them in my room, privately, and just soak in the lyrics lying on the floor. If strength returned, I'd sing along with them.

One such song that sticks out to me from an especially dark season of depression is *Keep Singing* by MercyMe. I encourage you to look up the song and listen to it.

One phrase that stood out was about Jesus singing over me. When I'd listen to this song, I could picture myself, curled up in Jesus' lap, allowing Him to sing over me with healing words. With that song and others. I would just soak in the songs, their healing lyrics, and allow Him to minister to me. The lyrics also encouraged me to keep going and eventually push through the depression.

You probably have your own slate of songs you go to when you need encouragement. I suggest that if you don't already have one, build a play list of songs that speak to your situation. Then sit, soak, and listen. Trust God to minister to you through His anointed kids who penned those songs, and wrote those melodies.

I'd like to share a short list of some of my

favorites. But also understand each season of trials is going to demand different types of encouragement. Different songs and lyrics.

For example, if you've lost someone close to you, you may want to find songs that are encouraging about loss, grief, and heaven.

If you need encouragement to get through a season where you have obstacles, you may want to find songs with themes of being an overcomer.

Here are some of my favorites to listen to when I need God to encourage me that I can make it through a tough time. That He's got a plan no matter how bad things look. Specifically that He will bring good from trials (Romans 8:28). These also encourage me to praise Him in the midst of a tough time.

You're Gonna Be Okay (Jenn Johnson)
Thy Will (Hillary Scott)
Small Enough (Nichole Nordeman)
Lift Me Up (The Afters)
Glorious Unfolding (Steven Curtis Chapman)
Broken Hallelujahs (The Afters)
Bitter Sweet (Amanda Cook)
Mended (Matthew West)
You Are I Am (MercyMe)
Save Me (Steffany Gretzinger)
Sound of Surviving (Nichole Nordeman)

I put that last one because it's like a triumphant march out of depression, a turning point with its upbeat tempo. I encourage you to not only fill your lists with tear-jerking songs, but these songs of triumph as well that fit your theme. (You can also strategically choose the order that you listen to these songs in, so they progress emotionally.)

And here's a tip: If you watch the songs on a computer or on your phone, finding the lyric videos helps to make sure you can absorb all the words. But it's also nice sometimes to just close your eyes and absorb. I like to do this date both ways.

The sample list is just one of my lists. I could come up with many different ones to suit various emotional situations. Loss, grief, the need for surrender. (Matt Redman's *Gracefully Broken* is great for a surrender theme.) Perhaps you want a set of songs about repentance. Or one about the need to trust Him again. How about the need to fall in love with him again? (*Sing My Way Back* by Steffany Gretzinger is a great song for this setting and fits this book's theme well.)

As you can see, each situation could benefit from a different set of songs.

If you are in a particularly emotional season, alone in a room soaking with your eyes closed may be the best way to do this. But if you have to go out on a prayer walk just to get some privacy, consider only using your earpiece in one ear. Stay aware of your surroundings.

It's your turn to make your playlist that fits your *current* needs. Ask God to lead you to songs that will minister to your hurting heart. Then play them.

Soak. Listen. Let God heal you.

If you ever find yourself in another hard season in the future, return to this same song list or make a new one to fit your new issues. This is a great way to battle through it with Jesus, instead of alone.

Journal about how you feel. Even if it's ugly and emotional and "wrong." Let Him come in and heal those parts of you.

After all the songs play, capture any words you feel the Lord speaks.

Be encouraged, knowing He loves to sing over you, even rejoice over you:

Zephaniah 3:17
"The Lord your God is with you, the Mighty Warrior who saves. He will take great delight in you; in His love He will no longer rebuke you, but will rejoice over you with singing."

Date 13
Let's Go to the Movies

Location: Your home in a room with a television or at a
   movie theater
Supplies: None
Reading: Read chapter before your date

$\mathcal{B}$eing a moviemaker, you knew I'd have to work in
a movie date night, right?

Movie night in, movie night out. Doesn't matter.
Either way it's fun, or it can be a meaningful,
emotional ride.

For this date, I am going to suggest you choose
a movie that is specifically from the faith-based
camp of movies or one you know has Bible friendly
themes, at the very least. I know there are many

movies that may contain some mainstream content that we can get a lot out of message wise. But for this date, I'd love for you to keep this in the realm of Philippians 4:8:

> "Finally, brothers and sisters, whatever is true, whatever is noble, whatever is right, whatever is pure, whatever is lovely, whatever is admirable — if anything is excellent or praiseworthy — think about such things."

During this date, I want you to think on these things. Some mainstream movies often edge up their content in a way that may not match this list.

My preference on this date is to find a movie that is currently in theaters. I love to support Christian filmmakers. However, if there isn't one out right now or one that you want to see, Netflix.com, PureFlix.com, and Amazon Prime or rentals should do just fine.

Allow me to make a few suggestions of those not currently in theaters. Most are from the top 100 grossing films in the Christian category. (Okay, admittedly, some of them are self-serving, works of mine or close friends.)

Overcoming Obstacles / Inspirational:
I Can Only Imagine

The Ultimate Gift
Soul Surfer
Champion
When the Game Stands Tall
Woodlawn
Facing the Giants
I'm Not Ashamed

Saving Marriages:
Fireproof
Extraordinary
Indivisible
The Song

Family:
Moms' Night Out
Like Arrows
October Baby
Courageous
The Grace Card

Prayer:
War Room

Heaven / Miracle Themes:
Miracles from Heaven
Heaven is for Real
90 Minutes in Heaven

Beliefs:
God's Not Dead
The Case for Christ

Allegorical:
The Chronicles of Narnia Series

Biblical / Historical:
The Passion of the Christ
Paul the Apostle
Son of God
Risen
The Nativity Story
One Night with the King

Choose your movie, either to watch at home or in the theater. When it's over, get in a quiet place with your journal.

Answer the following:

- How did that story make me feel?
- What is the biblical message here? (A verse or theme?)
- How does this theme apply to my life right now?
- Is there anything God may want me to do in response to having lived through this story with Him by my side tonight?

If you went to see a movie about saving marriages, did it encourage you to want to make amends with your spouse about something or inspire a new habit you'd like to develop?

If the movie was about a character reaching a dream, did it inspire you to think about a dream you've let go? One you feel like you should go for again?

If the movie showed a character dealing with a difficult situation yet ultimately not losing their faith, did it inspire you to want to relate to God in the same way?

Jesus often spoke in parables. He liked to use stories to reach people. I believe Christian writers are modeling His example when they write stories today in films and novels. Stories that can touch hearts and minds.

When I went to see *Soul Surfer*, I was so excited to see a true story where a young person took a horrible situation she'd been through and used it to help other people. She shared of her life with others. How she overcame obstacles and helped those in pain find hope. For me, Bethany Hamilton's story demonstrated Romans 8:28 in action. Seeing that movie was a good, biblical experience for me, highlighting the truth of one of my favorite verses. It challenged my faith in a good way.

So, let's go to the movies. With God. Hopefully, you will find this type of date also worth repeating.

Date 14
The Prayer Room

Location: A local prayer room, an IHOP, a 24-7 prayer
   room or a prayer room at your church
Supplies: Journal
Reading: Read whole chapter before your date

I've always enjoyed visiting prayer rooms. Some
are more creative than others. I've been to an
International House of Prayer. I've visited prayer
rooms at churches where they have a basic room
with a piano and chairs set apart for prayer
meetings. Mission retreat centers with prayer spaces.
Special buildings dedicated to prayer ministries,
some of which have prayer counselors on staff. And
a special prayer room called The Art Gallery, which

was by far my favorite. It had easels, paints, colored pencils for drawing (and to display on the walls). Walls covered in paper to write down prayers with pen or marker. Index cards to put prayer requests on and hang them from a string by a clothespin. It held rocks where you could write with a black Sharpie the names of unsaved family members or friends, and place that on a pile of other pretty rocks for everyone to pray for. Private nooks, corners, and lots of pillows, chairs and couches. Praise music available on a music player. It was an incredibly peaceful place to be. I wish every town had one.

My husband and I recently visited a prayer room called The Upper Room. They have little booths where you can have a room to yourself with a chair and dim lighting, to encourage you to sit alone and pray. They have a main room for organized prayer meetings as well.

My hope is that somewhere near you, there is some kind of prayer room to visit. Find out where one is, research it. Make sure it's affiliated with a Christian church or ministry. If it sounds like a good environment, pack up your book, journal, pen and a prayerful heart. Earmark time to spend with the Lord in a place that is blanketed with the Holy Spirit's presence, where other prayer warriors have been before you.

Once you are there, let God guide that prayer time. What you do will depend on what the space itself offers. (Artwork, places to put prayer requests, ways to pray for others' needs.) Try to mix up your time praying for your needs plus the needs of others, including the strangers whose needs have been posted.

As you may remember from Volume 1, I suggested coming up with a *War Room* in the style of a bulletin board, where you write prayer requests for yourself and others and tack them to the board. That was my way of making my own prayer space at home. But hopefully for this date, you can join what someone else is already doing and get away from home.

Try to make sure you find time for yourself and God alone. This is a date after all. But also don't be afraid to try an organized event in one of these places. Sometimes, if they have an event, they will also have some praise and worship groups playing to sit and listen to. Sometimes there are staff members to pray with you. There is power in prayer. Much can be accomplished taking this time with God.

James 5:14-16
"Is anyone among you sick? Then he must call for the elders of the church and they are to pray over him, anointing him with oil in the name of the Lord; and the prayer offered in faith will restore the one who is sick, and

the Lord will raise him up, and if he has committed sins, they will be forgiven him. Therefore, confess your sins to one another, and pray for one another so that you may be healed. The effective prayer of a righteous man can accomplish much."

Philippians 4:6-7

"Be anxious for nothing, but in everything by prayer and supplication with thanksgiving let your requests be made known to God. And the peace of God, which surpasses all comprehension, will guard your hearts and your minds in Christ Jesus."

Regardless of when you go, let God lead your time. Your prayers.

What a neat way to foster intimacy with Him, going to "His" house to meet with Him.

Date 15
Divine Priorities

Location: A quiet place, at home is probably best or somewhere you can type

Supplies: A computer or laptop, your calendar

Reading: Read chapter during your date

Exodus 20:3 makes it clear. "You shall have no other gods before me."

God is a jealous God; He likes attention. He wants to be our number one priority. Not second, not third and certainly not tenth on our list.

This date is about looking at your priorities and setting things straight if needed.

We are not likely to be able to do an hour for hour match for time given to God vs. other priorities. He is graceful about that. He knows we have husbands to focus on, bills to pay, jobs to go to, and kids to raise. Those are God-given blessings (and responsibilities). So it's not an either-or thing. It's not like God has nothing to do with those priorities, right? This is where quality has to trump quantity in our relationship. But still...let's take time today to look at what takes up our time. Ask God to help us decide if there's anything on our list that needs to be taken off, or if there's anything that needs to be added on.

Let's look at the main areas of life that take up our time and demand attention. You may have areas that don't fit the categories I'll list next, so feel free to add yours to the list. I'm just listing some broad categories.

1) God, Jesus, Holy Spirit
2) Family (spouse, kids, immediate family)
3) Friends
4) Work
5) Household
6) Future dreams and goals
7) Church
8) Ministry / Volunteer work
9) Rest
10) Leisure, Play Time

You can write a list like this one. Or you can be creative and use a program that lets you draw circles with various spokes coming out of each one. You can start with a global priority and then draw circles for ideas that go with that priority. I did one for our future marriage ministry, *Finally One*. I'll share the design for illustrative purposes.

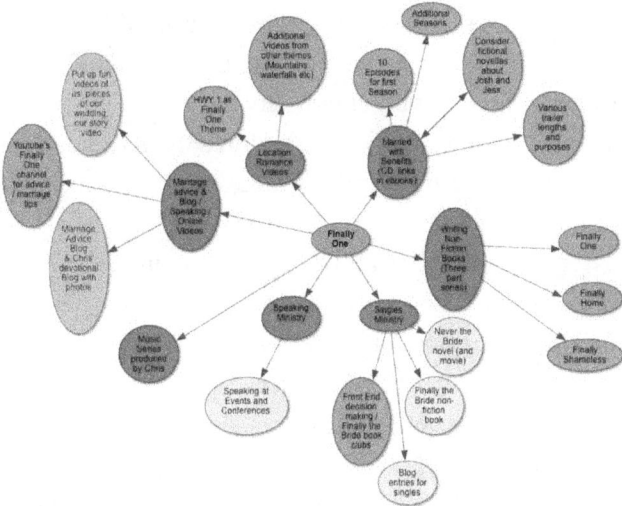

I also did this for my writing work one time. Writing up a list of main projects, sequels, prequels, books, movies, kids programs and picture books. A mix of fiction and nonfiction. Everything I wanted to accomplish. Sometimes it helps to see these things written out visually. If you are a visual planner, you can use this format.

Once you write up your list that includes all of my broad categories plus your own, take a look at your calendar. Try to figure out how much time you need to keep up with each one. Does one area take over more than it should? Is one area being neglected?

Then evaluate what those priorities have to do with your love relationship with God. Where does going on these dates fit in? Where does Bible reading or prayer time or ministering to others fit? How much church involvement do you have time for? Not just attending services and events. Are you able to give of your time and resources there? Should you do more or less?

Our church has a philosophy I really appreciate. The pastors are of the heart and mind to say, "I want to join in support of what you are doing and your calling" instead of trying to get us to fit into what they are doing, what their ministry is. I have found this to be freeing. They are big on supporting where God is leading us, instead of just trying to make sure they have a warm body at an event.

When I recently looked at my priorities, I realized Bible reading wasn't one of them. I had gotten slack. To help with this, my husband and I started a reading plan. We can't do it every single day. (It's set up to be about 5-6 chapters in a single reading.) But we do sit together, read at the same time, then discuss it when we're done. This has allowed for accountability and fostering a habit we'd gotten out of.

As that circle-filled chart showed, we also have a desire to build a marriage ministry called *Finally One*. We even have the website and some video curriculum that we've shot. But writing the books has been tough. Thankfully, I've been getting consistent work as a screenwriter, which naturally takes priority. My husband has been working as an editor and videographer. We recently talked about how we could continue to progress in our book and video series, even if it was just a little time each month.

Do you have spiritual habits you need to add back into your life? Do you need to give up that last TV show at the end of the night to fit it in? Notice I do put leisure on my list. We need downtime. We need breaks. Not just sleep but times of fun.

I hope today's exercise has allowed you to pinpoint where you may need to dial back from some activities and what types you should add back in.

Like every activity in this book, I pray this has been God-led, that you are sensitive to His voice in setting your priorities. Remember: lovers spend time together and make each other a priority. This should include our Creator, the Lover of Our Souls. Give Him your first fruits, not your leftovers.

Vision Board Date

Location: At home

Supplies: Magazines, poster board, colored markers or access to a website like Pinterest

Reading: Read whole chapter during your date

*T*his date is a springboard after the last one on priorities. But now, it's time to dream. In living color.

This date takes time to look at one of those priorities on that list:

Your future dreams. Your goals.

You can choose to make a vision board on poster board if you'd like. Or if you are a minimalist who doesn't like doing crafty projects, starting a new board on a website like Pinterest is a great alternative.

When you formed your list of priorities, you wrote down ideas for "future dreams and goals." What items made that list? You are going to make a vision board with various symbols or pictures representing all of those dreams that haven't come to fruition yet. Maybe you've started to work toward those. Or maybe you are at square one. It doesn't matter. What matters is that you believe you have a dream worth reaching.

Proverbs 29:18 (kjv)
"Where there is no vision, the people perish: but he that keepeth the law, happy *is* he."

I was blessed to grow up in a family where following dreams was encouraged. My parents are big dreamers and always told me I could do it. No matter what "it" was. (Yes, even when I said I wanted to be an actress. Though my talent didn't match my desires. God had to redirect me to writing where it was His heart for me to work.)

I am a firm believer in God giving us dreams. (Even though God's vision for me was to be a writer, not an actress.) I am one of those who believes God blesses us with talents. He wants us to use those talents for *His glory*, not our own.

Did you catch that? His glory.

Sometimes, the wait to see those come to fruition is tied to Him molding and shaping our character to ready us to handle the responsibility.

Do you believe God gave you a specific dream or vision for your life? This is a great time to ask before you embark on making this board. It takes discernment. Not every desire we come up with is God-led.

Do you feel like He's giving you clearance to dream this specific aspiration? Clearance to make a plan toward it?

God gives us ideas and inspiration. None of that happens by accident. He even planned dreams for us long before we were born. We were all meant to fill a need here. And it's our calling to do what we were designed to do.

Ephesians 2:10
"For we are God's handiwork, created in Christ Jesus to do good works, which God prepared in advance for us to do."

Now we just need to check in with God, on this date, and make sure we're striving toward the right works. Those He prepared in advance.

Some goals and dreams take longer or take harder work to become part of our realities. Meanwhile, we need motivation. That's what having a vision board is for. It gives you a physical representation of your goals.

You can cut out photos from magazines or newspapers or whatever you can find that has pictures that match your dreams. Since you're on a date with Him, ask God to lead you to the right images and phrases as well. You can cut out words and letters to put specific words on your board. Or you can draw them. (If you can draw, maybe you can use fancy lettering people use on chalkboards these days. I, however, cannot do that very well — try as I might, when I got a chalkboard and colored liquid markers for Christmas this past year.)

If you use a site like Pinterest, you can do a search for items that match your specific dream.

Had I made a vision board for writing, I could have posted pictures on my board of things like a completed script, a published novel, a New York Times Best-Selling list, or a top-grossing list of films. Pictures of Post-It notes, links of articles on how to be a better writer, inspiring quotes. Anything to motivate me. Keep me focused. I could even have posted pictures that represented future ideas for stories I'd like to tell. (Like of locations of various settings.)

I have vision boards for specific writing projects. For example, I have one about Danish heritage as research for a future book series, *Windmill Falls*. I made them for projects like *Song of Springhill*, saving mining themed photos and Canada posts and historical information about what happened during those mining disasters in Nova Scotia. It was my inspiration when writing the novel. I made a Christmas board to show cute little Christmas towns to inspire my novella and screenplay, *O Little Town of Bethany*.

This date is meant to build an overview board. One that encompasses your biggest dreams that haven't come true yet.

Don't forget to include inspiring quotes too. "Don't give up" themes or about persistence. Make it colorful and fun.

If it's something you make on poster board, put it somewhere that you can see it, to remind yourself to keep going for it. If it's online, visit the site sometimes, pray over it.

Again, like the Word of God says, if we don't have vision, we perish. Our dreams die. It's a sad state of mind if we stop dreaming, stop hoping.

This brings me to an important part of this process. Are you sure your dream is God-given and not self-driven? Not driven by selfish motives? (In my industry, people's dreams are often tied to wanting to be famous. God may not allow that dream to come true until that person is ready to handle it in a less prideful way or until they adopt a purer motive.)

Look over your board. Ask God for any adjustments. Does anything need to come off? Also, ask Him if anything is missing.

These boards can grow and change over time. You can make more for different types of dreams. Or you can add to the one you have. Especially if God is inspiring you in a new way or shows you something that belongs on it. The point is to be open to Him. You are, after all, on a date with Him as you make this board.

Let God fill your vision with His dreams and goals for your life. Then walk arm-in-arm with Him to reach them.

To Be a Kid Again

Location: A kids' park

Supplies: None

Reading: Read whole chapter before your date

One of the greatest joys of my adult life is going on roller coasters with my parents. My seventy-something parents. Still going on rides, still acting like kids at Disney World. Still wanting to play and goof off with me.

Sometimes, I think this joy my heart feels to see them still "young at heart" gives me a mere glimpse at Jesus' joy. He loves to see us come to Him like children.

This may sound strange. But one of my favorite

dates with God was my visit to a park with lots of stuff for kids to do.

Swings, slides, things to climb.

There was a time in my life when a friend was praying for me, saying I needed to learn to just be a kid with God again. To have fun with Him again. I took that to heart. I set out to spend time with Him in a new, childlike way.

What better way than to get out and play? (No one has to know what you're doing at that park, right?) A park that happens to not be busy when you go is highly preferred. So, a weekday is likely to work best while kids are at school. Naturally, I don't suggest at night, alone, when it's dark. Safety first.

Also, it's not a bad idea to pay attention to signs so you don't get in trouble. Some parks, especially in California, have signs that request adults stay out of play yards, if you're not there watching a child. (And you don't count, even if you're acting like one!) This is to keep people from getting spooked by your presence. (If I could convince McDonalds I was short enough to go in their bubble pools, I would!)

This one park I visited had a lake, a dock, a beachfront, swings, slides, one of those spinny wheels that make you feel sick if you go too fast for too long. Because I was there alone and to spend time with God, it felt very playful, like we were sharing a secret. Like having a carefree time with a good buddy. We didn't have to talk about anything serious — or even talk at all. We could take time to just "be" and laugh, of course.

In my own neighborhood, there are times when no one is at our kids' park. But I rather enjoy finding other parks where I won't run into anyone I know. (What if I get caught praying out loud as I try to get that swing to go higher and higher toward heaven?)

So why should we go on this date? Why act like a child? Jesus often talks about how wonderful children are, how He loves when they come to Him with that childlike faith.

Also, doesn't Jesus ask us — as adults — to come to Him like children?

Matthew 18:3, 10
"And He said: 'Truly I tell you, unless you change and become like little children, you will never enter the kingdom of heaven... See that you do not despise one of these little ones. For I tell you that their angels in heaven always see the face of My Father in heaven.'"

This sounds like a great excuse to become a kid again. And it's fun. Trust me, you'll enjoy it. You may feel silly at first. But there's something freeing about soaring on a swing. Something that brings you back to a more innocent time in life.

Here are some sample pictures from that date:

Take some selfies to commemorate this time later, to put into your *Dates with God* scrapbook. (Help me not be the only one!)

Become childlike again, with childlike faith, and enjoy that date with God.

Date 18
To Climb a Mountain

Location: A mountain or hiking location
Supplies: Water, journal, Bible
Reading: Read chapter before your date

Nature dates are big for me in this volume and Volume 1. Nothing makes me feel closer to God than getting out in His creation. This one has a specific spin on it.

This one allows you to prayerfully do something symbolic on your date. An action that means something just to you.

What figurative mountains are you facing in life right now? What big obstacles or challenges?

Mark 11:23

"Truly I tell you, if anyone says to this mountain, 'Go, throw yourself into the sea,' and does not doubt in their heart but believes that what they say will happen, it will be done for them."

Even Jesus used the word mountain to symbolize a challenge or an obstacle. Let this date be about praying about that issue — that "mountain" or obstacle — as you walk up.

If your health allows, try climbing to the top. But naturally don't overdo it. There may be an overlook you can aim for that's halfway up.

In California, there was a small mountain in Burbank. I could walk to the top in about 30 minutes. It was strenuous because it was mostly uphill. I'd bring a bag with a journal, water, a small Bible, and a pen. I'd sit up there and take a break — take my date with God — before heading back down.

Normally, when I'd head up this mountain, I was dealing with something in particular I wanted to pray about.

Today, having that agenda on your date is okay. It's part of the purpose. Go on this date knowing it's time to pray through this "mountain" or challenge in your life.

It may not be something fixable in one hike. But this could be a good start. A place you can return to, to continue to contend for whatever the prayer need is.

Bring a journal and Bible (electronically on your phone will be easier), take time at the top to sit. Read. Ask God to bring you to any specific Scriptures that may speak to your situation. Write down anything you sense.

For this example I'm choosing a mountain, as it's often a normal symbol used for challenges we face. You can also change up this date idea if you can think of something that better fits your personal situation. (Or another area that symbolizes obstacles for you.)

Here's another spin on the mountain date. Do you feel like you're walking around the same mountain, having to sludge through the same lessons from God, over and over? I must admit, this has happened to me more than once. (And yes, like the Israelites in the desert, I'd complain. I'd get stuck in a "forty year lesson" I should have learned in two weeks.) Maybe you can take some time to walk around part of that mountain's bottom, pray, then make your way to the top as a symbol of breakthrough.

Do this however you feel led. Thankfully, you are not alone in tackling this obstacle. Your Date is with you.

Date 19
To Book a Date

Location: A quiet place

Supplies: A nonfiction, Christian book (not including this one or the Bible), one you haven't started to read yet but that speaks to current issues in life

Reading: Read this whole chapter before your date

As we know, reading the Bible needs to be a higher priority than reading other nonfiction books. Our best wisdom from God comes from His Book. However, sometimes, it's good to share in someone else's wisdom for a topic. The Holy Spirit still inspires book writers.

For this date, I want you to choose a new book you haven't read yet. Make it nonfiction. A book you're hoping can speak to your current life situation or can help you grow closer to God.

If you are struggling with or asking questions about something in particular, I encourage you to search on that topic and find a book that is from a Christian perspective on that topic. For example, if you are struggling to face and heal from past abuse, I encourage you to read Christa Sands' *Learning to Trust Again*.

If you just want to learn something deeper about God, find a book that covers that. For example, if you want to learn more about God speaking through dreams, I encourage you to pick up a copy of Mark Virkler and Charity Virkler Kayembe's book, *Hearing God Through Your Dreams*. If you want to grow in praying for your husband, I recommend *The Power of a Praying Wife* by Stormie Omartian.

Get someplace quiet, away from others, where you can read the first couple of chapters.

Then ask God what He'd like you to glean from this reading today. What does the message of this book, thus far, have to do with you, your life, your faith?

Put in your journal the insights you sense He gives you. After today's date, set a time when you'll resume. Repeat as many times as needed until you finish the book. But make this a special and set apart time between you and God. Not just something you do right before you fall asleep at night. Especially if the book you chose is something that's on your heart to wrestle with.

Let God speak through the wisdom of others.

Date 20
God's Choice

Location: To be determined
Supplies: To be determined
Reading: Read chapter before your date

*J*ust think... The relationship you're building with God means He can ask you on a date, anywhere, anytime.

And that means now. This is not the same as Reader's Choice, which will come soon enough with Date 23, where you get to design your own date in the form of an idea I haven't suggested.

This one is driven by God. *And it's an idea you do not know yet. You have to pray first.*

Have you ever been on a date where your suitor

did not tell you where you were going but just told you what to bring and how to dress?

I had one of those on February 18, 2011, with my then boyfriend Chris Price. He picked out the clothes he thought I should wear when what I first put on wasn't exactly the best choice. Ratty old jeans I'd had for about 10 years with embroidered flowers on them and a matching pastel sweater. So I let him choose another outfit. Still casual but nicer. He also told me to bring a jacket because it was supposed to rain a bit. This tipped me off some of our day would be outside.

I didn't know it but we were heading down to my favorite spot in Southern California: the Santa Monica Pier. On our way, we picked up a photographer—the one I didn't know was joining us—who was going to take "couples photos" of us for the day. Yes, I got ready for this date having no idea I was about to be part of a photo shoot. That was part of "the big surprise" for our date.

I was thankful he told me what to wear because we got over 400 photos taken by the wonderful Lisa Crates that day. Those pictures turned into our engagement photos, all caught on camera live as it unfolded. (Trust me: I would not have been happy if had I worn my first set of casual clothes. No thanks. I'm glad my date, Chris, knew to tell me to wear something else.)

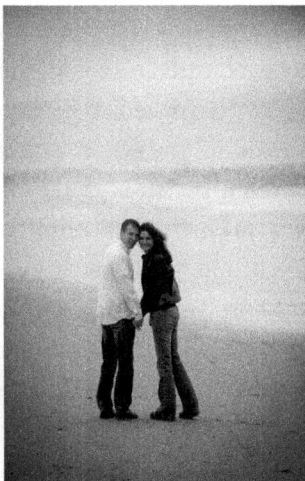

So in the same way, this next date is *God's choice*. Before you go anywhere, ask Him what you will need to bring and a general sense of where you may be going. (You can also ask Him what He'd like you to wear.) Location and weather appropriate, right?

See what idea He lights up on your mind. For example, if you weren't thinking about food and a restaurant pops into your head, maybe He's summoning you out to dinner. Listen for that "still small voice."

If you read *25 Dates With God* Volume 1, you may recall the day I went on a walk, asked God where I should go and He'd led me to a new street. I wasn't sure why He wanted me to walk up that steep hill. But upon arrival at this crazy, dilapidated house that was decorated like my childhood home, I knew what I was there for. I knew what God wanted to accomplish in me that day. Without a doubt I knew He'd led me there and that He wanted to speak to me—specifically about some things that had happened at that home I needed to heal from.

If God doesn't light a specific idea on your mind for a date and instead encourages you to get in the car and drive, do it. Don't be afraid. Be open.

You never know what fun adventure may be awaiting you. (Bring a camera!) And don't get lost. Drive safely and listen for His prompts.

This reminds me of a story I read in a minister's autobiography where he talked about walking in cornfields on his family's farm as a child. He'd purposefully get lost in them, then pray about how to find his way out. He said this was his training on how to hear God's voice as God would tell him to turn left or right at the proper moments.

Let this be that type of adventure for you, going on a new date you've not been on so far that God inspires you to do.

During the writing of this book, I wanted another example for this chapter. So I asked God to lead me somewhere for a date.

I felt like I should try out a new, paved trail in town that had piqued my curiosity but I'd never been to before. Ironically, though, because it was a rather industrial area and behind neighborhoods but didn't connect to any, I didn't feel 100% safe. It was secluded with just one path. The only way out of it was to backtrack.

Even though I knew God was with me, I still walked with the watchfulness I'd learned in my Safety and Awareness class. I'll admit: it was a bit distracting. It wasn't the most peaceful date I'd ever been on. I always want us to be aware of safety concerns. Especially as women.

In spite of that, this date had its meaningful moments. During the walk through new territories, I would arrive at places that were beautiful. Paved paths that wound through the tall and exceptionally green trees. They were stunning! It was nearing the end of spring when the greenery had finally returned. Yet it's a much more vibrant color compared to late summer.

Ironically, the area was also full of turtles. At one point, I saw five or six of them on a rock. (Unfortunately they slipped off the rock when a squirrel distracted them, before I could snag a picture.)

One of the things I felt led to pray about during this "God's Choice Date" was the frustration that I had no idea what to expect about a particular issue I was facing. Plus, it was a situation that was progressing extremely slowly! (Can you say "turtle speed"?) I didn't like the unknown; it had been driving me a bit crazy. And one of those beautiful paths showed a bend in the road where I couldn't see ahead. I felt like God was using it as an illustration to say He knew how I felt. He was acknowledging my sense of not being able to "see" ahead.

Once I continued my walk, I could see beyond that bend. And you know what? It was really odd. Not much further down, the path just suddenly ended.

It didn't go anywhere like I thought it did.

Didn't connect anywhere.

It actually stopped at a paved circle where you had to turn around and head back the way you came. In a way, despite the beauty, it felt disappointing.

Ironically, the issue I was praying about, ended up concluding a couple of days later in the same way.

Disappointing.

It didn't land where I wanted it to land. Felt like a closed door that dead-ended.

Perhaps this date was preparation for my heart before the real life event unfolded. I did not leave that prayer time with any degree of "hope" it would turn out well. If anything, I felt like it would turn out badly.

And it did, those few days later. My heart hurt, for sure.

But that doesn't take away from God's time with me, His kindness in preparing my heart. It's not a path I feel compelled to return to, like I had hoped.

So, while that may not be a happy ending, these dates are about having a real relationship. The outcome of the real life situation isn't God's fault. But He did prepare me. And for that, I'm grateful.

So now it's your turn.

Ask God where you should go. Take His hand and trust Him to lead.

Keep notes about anything He shows you. Take pictures. After all, if it's His idea, it may turn out to be one of your most meaningful dates yet.

Date 21
A Dream Date

Location: In bed right after a dream

Supplies: Journal

Reading: Read chapter before your date, to prepare for the next time He sends you a dream

$\mathcal{D}$o you believe that God still speaks through dreams today? I'm thankful there is no evidence that He stopped with the Bible.

If anything, He lets us know this practice will continue until the end of the age.

Acts 2:17
"In the last days, God says, I will pour out my Spirit on all people. Your sons and

daughters will prophesy, your young men will see visions, your old men will dream dreams."

I'm thankful to have had many moments in my life when God has spoken through dreams. A warning, a word of encouragement. Even sometimes a slice of humor. (Yes, God does have a sense of humor. He invented laughter.)

The tricky part is that once you get a dream that captures your attention, how do you make sure you listen before it fades from memory?

Make it a Dream Date with God. Write it down immediately.

This is one of the only dates that has to be upon waking, first thing in the morning (or in the middle of the night if that's when God wakes you up). If you don't capture it right away, you will most likely forget. And who wants to forget a message from their Beloved Date?

God has woken me up many times at 3:33 a.m. to get me to write down a dream. It's like our little code. I know it's Him when it's that time on the clock. When I was single, I could sit up and turn the light on. Now I have to sneak into the bathroom with a journal so I don't wake up Chris.

Sometimes, I wasn't sure what the dream meant when I started writing it down. But God was able to speak to me in my obedience of writing it down first.

Then He would help me understand its symbolism.

I encourage you to do the same. There isn't room in this book to teach dreams and how to look at them fully. (I mentioned a great book by the Virklers, *Hearing God Through Your Dreams*. That's a great place to start if this is a new concept for you.)

In the meantime, I suggest if you get a dream that feels significant, write it down. Just the details of the dream itself first. Then write how you felt, and write any thoughts you have about what area of life it may be referring to.

Take your quiet time with God to allow Him to speak about it.

Mark Virkler was on the Sid Roth show, *It's Supernatural*, talking about God speaking through dreams. He told a story about me on the show, about the time I got a dream that let me know one of my friends was suicidal. The dream also indicated this person was in a lock down, mental facility. Imagine my surprise when I went looking for this friend the next day. Upon trying to reach her, I found out her friends brought her to a hospital where she could be watched for 72 hours because they feared she would kill herself.

I was so thankful God told me to find her through that dream. I would not have known she was in serious emotional trouble if God hadn't sent me that dream. We didn't live in the same state and I wouldn't have seen her until the holidays.

Once her friends at work told me where they brought her, I called the medical facility and asked if they would let me talk to her. To my surprise, they said yes.

Here's the loving thing God did and why this is such a beautiful story. When they got her on the phone, one of her first questions for me was, "How did you even know to look for me?" I told her God told me. That God had sent me a dream to let me know she was in trouble.

You can't imagine how much this meant to her. It communicated to her that God and people do care about her. She wasn't forgotten. That someone noticed she was missing right away. Especially because the night before, her husband (now ex-husband) had told her that if she had died, no one would notice or care. And yet here, God was undercutting that terrible lie. I knew she was "missing" within one day. Because God, in His loving kindness, sent me that dream.

My time with God, figuring out what this dream meant then having prayer time for my friend, was so meaningful—not to mention life changing and important.

I encourage you to do the same. Start listening to your dreams. Spend time with God, ask Him what they mean and what you should learn from them. Many dreams are just for you to learn from. Not all of them will be life-or-death situations about family or friends. You may get a mix of both.

Sometimes, He may point out a sin issue in your life through a dream. Or He may want to encourage an area of your heart that He knows is in pain. All we have to do is be open, be willing to write down dreams, and listen.

The way I organize my dreams when I journal about them is to look at them like mini-movies. I look at them from a story perspective.

I write down the following:

- Genre (ex. thriller, comedy, drama)
- Dream Story (what it was about)
- Dream Subtext (what it might mean, including symbols used, what they may represent)
- God's Theme (what I feel God is saying)
- Self-Revelation (how it seems to apply to my life right now or the life of whoever it's about)

One day I plan to publish a book on dreams and God speaking through them. But until then, this short overview will have to do.

I hope you will enjoy a date or two or five with God as He speaks to you this visionary way.

Date 22
The Buddy System

Location: A place out in nature or a good walking
  location
Supplies: A good friend
Reading: Read chapter before your date

*I*magine a night where you and a friend have the
same date. Scandalous, right?

Not in this case.

Have you ever thought of inviting someone into
the *Dates With God* process?

I'm talking about a buddy. A good friend.

For the moment, especially if you are single, I'm
not suggesting you invite a romantic interest. Let's
keep the focus where it belongs, shall we?

One of my favorite traditions when I still lived in California was to go walking every Sunday with one of my best friends. We would walk our feet off for about five or six hours. We'd explore new streets and territory. Or we'd repeat our favorite walk on the beach strand. (Including that same pier where Chris would one day propose marriage to me.) We'd mix it up.

What didn't change is we always talked about deep things. What was going on in our lives. What was going on in our hearts. Often, this would lead to praying together. Sometimes on a bench alongside some beautiful flowers. Sometimes on the sand. Otherwise, just while walking. I'm sure it looked like we were just talking to each other. No one else had to know. I feel like these were some of my most important years, growing in the Lord, before I got married. We had lots of God encounters on these outings too.

So how about you? Got a friend in mind?

Maybe you have a friend whose relationship with God could use a boost. Maybe you have a friend who's on fire for God but may not have thought about taking these fun, adventurous dates with God. Maybe you have a mentor who's stronger in the Lord than you are, but one you think would enjoy something like this.

Once you settle on the person you'd like to invite, think about your friend's interests. What do they like to do? Do they enjoy a good walk on the beach? A stroll down a nature trail? Time spent sitting on a rock in front of a waterfall?

Try to pick an activity that you think that friend would enjoy. But make sure—embedded in your idea for a buddy date—is a place you could have some quiet time. Together and separately.

Privacy will help you include some prayer time.

Extend an invite to this friend. Tell them about what this journey has been like, since you started dating God. Give them a few examples of encounters you've had with God on this journey so far or about your favorite date. Ask if they'd like to join you for a Buddy System Date.

If appropriate, pack a lunch. Make a fun day of it if you'd like. But earmark part of your day together for time with God alone and time together when you'll focus on God.

Let them know the plan, where you'll go and what you'll do. Encourage them to bring a journal and pen they can easily carry wherever you're going. Feel free to use a Bible app on your phone, if that helps, rather than carrying a Bible.

Then go out on this date to your chosen destination.

First, spend some time walking and praying together. As mentioned, it'll look like you're talking to each other. So if you encounter other walkers or hikers, they won't know the difference. Pray for God to meet you here today.

Take some time to praise Him. Praise welcomes His presence.

Then pray for each other's needs. (If you need a catch up time first, to update each other on what prayer needs you may have, feel free to work that in first.)

After a time praying together, go your separate ways to continue your date with the same Man.

Find different spots to sit quietly before God, holding your journal, and be ready to write down anything you feel He says to you. Feel free to ask God to speak to you on behalf of your friend.

This could include about their specific needs. Or it could just be asking God to give you a word of encouragement for them. This could include a Bible verse or just something He'd like to say. Even if you're not 100% sure of what you're writing down, just do it in faith. Your friend will be able to confirm for you if it bears witness to her spirit.

Just test it first yourself, to make sure whatever you write down is in line with the Bible. Nothing should contradict Scripture. Then see if it fits the basic rules of prophecy's purposes:

Encouragement, exhortation, and comfort. First Corinthians 14:1-3 puts it this way:

> "Follow the way of love and eagerly desire gifts of the Spirit, especially prophecy. For

anyone who speaks in a tongue does not speak to people but to God. Indeed, no one understands them; they utter mysteries by the Spirit. But the one who prophesies speaks to people for their strengthening, encouraging and comfort."

Then come back together and share thoughts with each other about what you prayed. Share whatever insights God gave you about yourself or your friend.

One time, a mentee of mine asked if we could do this for each other. Even though I was her mentor, she was volunteering to listen to God on my behalf and see if He wanted to share anything with her about me.

I'll never forget the way she blessed me that night and gave me a word of encouragement in an area of my life where I needed it. Wouldn't you love to do this for a friend?

While you could always do this at any time, at home, or on the phone, I suggest trying this under the context of concerted time with God, to get both of you focused on the same thing.

God and His love for us.

Assuming this date goes well, you may just be asking for a second date like this. And a third. Hanging out with friends doesn't only have to be going out shopping or out to eat or to movies, right?

Why not enjoy spending time with God together? You may just encourage this friend toward taking her own journey through *Dates With God*.

Maybe another time you can repeat this date with another friend.

A different variation on this date would be to get your small group or ladies' group involved in doing this together, like a little prayer retreat. You could help spread a movement toward encouraging women to seek deeper relationships with God.

Remember Matthew 18:20: "For where two or three gather in My name, there am I with them."

Date 23
Reader's Choice

Location: Your choice
Supplies: Your choice
Reading: Read whole chapter before your date

*H*as this second installment of the *Dates With God* series given you new ideas for dates with God that I haven't suggested? Now is the time to go on one of those.

Even if you wrote a list when going through the first installment, write another list now or add to the one you already started. It could be a new date from this book sparked fresh ideas for you. Choose one to go on now.

What do you need to make this date happen? Will it be inside, outside, at home or at some destination?

In any dating relationship, we enjoy sometimes letting our dates plan the outing. This is your chance to choose. Think about your interests, hobbies, and resources, and turn those into dates. You know the area where you live best. You may come up with ideas that I would never think of because I don't live where you do.

Go on your creative date. Take selfies and then, if you're willing, post about it with the #dateswithGod label on social media, like Twitter or Instagram. (If you use Twitter you can tag us at @purplepenworks.) You can also go to our website, **www.dateswithGod.com**, and leave a comment on the page for Volume Two of this series.

Feel free to just share your experience in a comment, or give us a link to where you've either blogged about your date or posted photos. By doing so, you will encourage others who are also "dating God" to have even more fun than they've had so far following my ideas. I don't pretend to be able to come up with every idea under the sun that we could enjoy on dates with God. So I want to welcome you into this process. I would love to try some of your ideas!

So, that's it. Easy enough, right? Write that list and take your first date from your list of ideas. In the future, revisit that list and try them all at least once.

And share with us how it goes!

Date 24
Scrapbooking Your Dates

Location: A place at home with a large table or desk
Supplies: A journal, your camera, computer, pictures from your dates, a scrapbook and supplies, or an online scrapbooking program
Reading: Read whole chapter before your date

We are getting close to the end of this second volume. Don't worry. If this has been an enjoyable process for you, this is just the second of at least three planned volumes. There will be more dates to come. I believe we should be dating God for the rest of our lives.

If you went through Volume One, you have begun some sort of scrapbook to commemorate your dates.

Before you get to the final date, where you will do a relationship check-in with God, I'd like you to use this date as a "look back" on all the dates you've been on so far in Volume Two. I've encouraged you along the way to take pictures. Pictures of things He's shown you, pictures of His beautiful artistry in nature, selfies of you on dates. Gather all of these pictures. Now it's time to add them to whatever scrapbook you started before. This date may take a few days or a week or so because it is a project.

As a reminder, just in case you didn't start that scrapbook yet, there are various approaches to this date you can take. You can choose to scrapbook your dates in a real live scrapbook with stickers and decorations. You can use a journaling photo album. You can start a blog about your dates, complete with photos. Or you can put together an online scrapbook. Either way, this is meant to be a faith-building exercise.

This project will continue to chronicle all the time you've spent with God since this journey began. Once you choose your method for scrapbooking, label your photos with what date number they were from out of this book, if you haven't already.

Remember to look up words in your journal that God said to you on each date. Pick out a special quote or piece of wisdom you feel He showed you on each date that goes with the pictures.

By now, you have probably had 23 new experiences with God that you haven't had before (Hopefully to add to the other 25). Save them and capture those memories.

Like any dating relationship, looking back on where we've been and the good times we've had is a fun activity. Especially if you have built good memories together. This date helps you do this visually, like you would capture in a wedding album. The next date will get into having some concentrated chat time with God to check in on your relationship.

Meanwhile, as you work through this project, I hope you enjoy your trip down memory lane.

.

Date 25
Relationship Check-In

Location: A quiet place
Supplies: A journal
Reading: Read chapter during your date

Congrats on making it this far, all the way to Date 25 of Volume Two. If you also went through Volume 1, that's 50 dates, now. Wow!

For this date, choose any location, perhaps even your favorite location from Dates 1-24 of this volume. It's time to do one of those "relationship check-ins."

I hope you've grown even more from the time you finished Volume 1.

I suggest you begin this date by reading your entries for your first date of Volume 1 and the first date of Volume 2. It never hurts to ask that question again: "Where are we in this relationship?"

I promise you that if you've been participating actively in these dates, your relationship is stronger than it was 24 dates ago.

Or 49 dates ago.

You've probably gotten to know more about God, His wonderful attributes, His personality, and His love for you. Your relationship has grown in intimacy. I hope your love for Him is exponentially higher. But it always helps to stop, take inventory, and check-in.

Remember that God loves you. He's already accepted you. There's nothing to be nervous about. He is more than happy to come to the table to chat with you about the state of your union. Lovers often talk about their relationship and all that makes it wonderful and unique. Spend time telling Him what this divine relationship means to you.

As you settle into your comfortable place, open your *Dates With God* journal.

- Do you feel closer to God than you did before you went on your first date of Volume 1?
- Do you feel even closer than when you started Volume 2? Are you continuing to progress?
- In what ways do you feel like you know God better?

- What was your favorite date of the 24 in this volume? Are there any you would like to repeat?
- What was your least favorite and why? Is it worth doing over?
- Have you found it easier to dialogue with God, the more time you spend with Him?
- In what ways did God show up on dates for you during this time that you hadn't experienced before?
- What are your future goals regarding your relationship with God?
- Make a plan: How would you like your dating relationship with God to continue?

Next, ask God a few questions and jot down anything you feel He says to you:

- Lord, how do you feel about our relationship now versus before?
- Have I grown?
- Where can I improve in my quest to know you better, Lord?
- Have I let anything come between You and me lately?
- Is there anything I'm not asking that you'd like to share with me?

Make a plan and schedule to keep going after you close this book. Naturally, you can always reread and revisit the dates in Volumes 1-2. I want to make sure this is an ongoing thing for you.

The goal of this book series is to help you establish a continuous relationship. I don't want you to finish this book (or any other volume) and stop dating God. If anything, I want this experience to have ignited a passion in you for Him, to kindle the flame that makes you want to go back to God over and over for these special dates.

Hopefully, this check-in results in that mutual decision to keep dating.

This part is *your* decision. Will you continue to invest in this relationship? Will you continue to play your part in how much it grows?

As a reminder: You are safe, you are accepted, and you are loved and wanted. Your spirit is safe with God. You are not abandoned by Him. This is the safest dating relationship you can ever be in. He will never leave you. Not even death can separate you from your True Love.

God is inviting you into greater intimacy. A greater, stronger love. A courtship unlike any other. So open your hand, accept His in yours, and enjoy a romance that can only be written by God.

About the Author

Cheryl McKay has been professionally writing since 1997. Tommy Nelson served as her first publisher, teaming her with Frank Peretti on the *Wild and Wacky, Totally True Bible Stories* series. Cheryl wrote the screenplay adaptation of *The Ultimate Gift*, the feature film starring Academy Award Nominees James Garner and Abigail Breslin. It's based on Jim Stovall's best-selling novel. The film was released by Fox in theaters in Spring 2007 and has won such awards as the Crystal Heart Award, the Crystal Dove, one of the Top Ten Family Movies at MovieGuide Awards, and a CAMIE Award. She also wrote the DVD for *Gigi: God's Little Princess*, another book adaptation based on the book by Sheila Walsh, and episodes of *Superbook*. She wrote a half-hour drama for teenagers about high school violence, called *Taylor's Wall*, produced in Los Angeles by Family Theater

Productions. After winning a fellowship, she was commissioned to write a feature script, *Greetings from the Flipside,* for Art Within, which Rene Gutteridge and McKay released as a novel through B&H Publishing in October 2013. Her screenplay, *Never the Bride,* was adapted into a novel by Gutteridge and was released by Waterbrook Press in June 2009. The film version is in development. As one passionate for those who are losing hope in their wait to find love, she released the nonfiction version, *Finally the Bride: Finding Hope While Waiting.* She also penned her autobiography, *Finally Fearless: Journey from Panic to Peace.* She wrote the screen story for *The Ultimate Life,* the sequel to *The Ultimate Gift.* McKay also co-wrote the films *Extraordinary* and *Indivisible,* both faith-based features. Find her on Facebook, Twitter, Pinterest, or at her websites:

www.purplepenworks.com
www.finallyone.com
www.dateswithGod.com

$\mathcal{D}$ear Readers:

Thank you for spending this time with me and more importantly with the God who loves you so much. I hope you will join me for other installments of this book series and take more dates with God.

If this book has been helpful to you, please recommend it to your friends and family. Would you mind leaving a review online where you purchased this book to share your thoughts with others?

Also, please visit our website and share your date experiences. (**www.dateswithGod.com**)

I wish you many blessings in your quest to know your loving Heavenly Father deeper and wider and more intimately.

Blessings,

Cheryl McKay

Dates With God Series:

Volume One: *Adventures in Faith*
Volume Two: *Courting Spiritual Intimacy*
Volume Three: *Falling in Love with Jesus*

Holiday Edition: Love Worth Celebrating

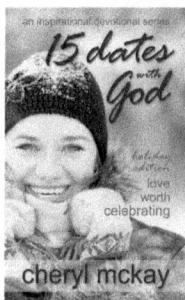

Finally the Bride

Finding Hope While Waiting

Cheryl McKay

Finally Fearless

Journey from Panic to Peace

How Overcoming Anxiety Helped Me Find True Love

cheryl mckay

Other Books by McKay

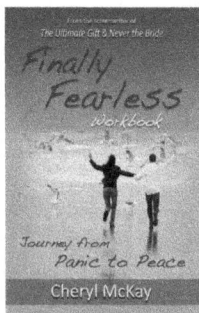

Finally Fearless Workbook
Journey from Panic to Peace
Cheryl McKay

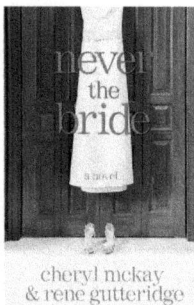

never the bride
a novel
cheryl mckay & rene gutteridge

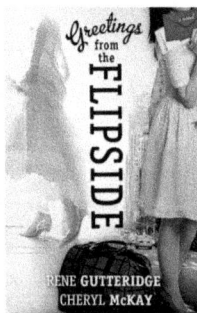

Greetings from the FLIPSIDE
RENE GUTTERIDGE
CHERYL McKAY

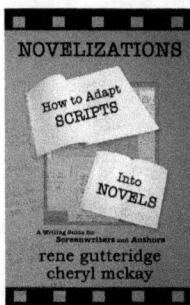

NOVELIZATIONS
How to Adapt SCRIPTS Into NOVELS
rene gutteridge
cheryl mckay

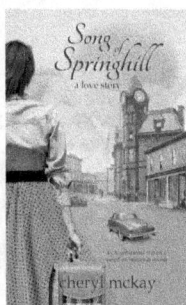

Song of Springhill
a love story
cheryl mckay

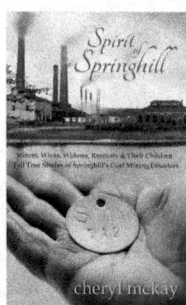

Spirit of Springhill
cheryl mckay

O Little Town of Bethany
rene gutteridge
cheryl mckay

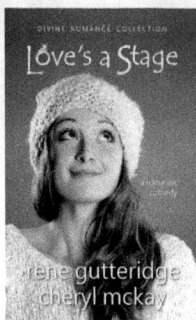

Love's a Stage
rene gutteridge
cheryl mckay

www.ingramcontent.com/pod-product-compliance
Lightning Source LLC
Chambersburg PA
CBHW072013040426
42447CB00009B/1608

From the co-author of *Never the Bride: a novel*

an inspirational devotional series

25 dates with God

volume two
courting
spiritual
intimacy

cheryl mckay

www.dateswithGod.com
#dateswithGod

Books by Cheryl McKay

Never the Bride: a novel (with Rene Gutteridge)
Finally the Bride: Finding Hope While Waiting
Finally Fearless: How Overcoming Anxiety Helped Me Find True Love
Song of Springhill: a love story
Spirit of Springhill: Miners, Wives, Widows, Rescuers & Their Children Tell True Stories of Springhill's Mining Disasters
Love's a Stage: a novel (with Rene Gutteridge)
O Little Town of Bethany: a novella (with Rene Gutteridge)
Greetings from the Flipside: a novel (with Rene Gutteridge)
Wild & Wacky, Totally True Bible Stories Series (children's books with Frank Peretti)

Films / Videos / Audio Dramas by Cheryl McKay

The Ultimate Gift (screenplay by)
The Ultimate Life (screen story by)
Extraordinary (co-writer)
Indivisible (co-writer)
Gigi: God's Little Princess DVD (screenplay)
Superbook (episode writer)
RiverKids (audio show writer)
Wild & Wacky Totally True Bible Stories Series (audio show writer)